Quinn and Penny INVESTIGATE How to RESEARCH

BY THOMAS KINGSLEY TROUPE

ILLUSTRATED BY SOLE OTERO

PICTURE WINDOW BOOKS
a capstone imprint

Thanks to our advisers for their expertise, research, and advice:

Diane Chen, Library Information Specialist
John F. Kennedy Middle School, Nashville, Tennessee

Terry Flaherty, PhD, Professor of English
Minnesota State University, Mankato

Photo Credits:
Capstone Studio: Karon Dubke, 11 (all); iStockphoto: Matt Craven, 20 (monster); Shutterstock: Jule_Berlin, 21 (castle), n. yanchuk, 20-21 (map), Rudolf Kotulán, 15 (castle)

Editor: Shelly Lyons
Designer: Lori Bye
Art Director: Nathan Gassman
Production Specialist: Sarah Bennett
The illustrations in this book were created digitally.

Picture Window Books
1710 Roe Crest Drive, North Mankato, MN 56003
www.capstonepub.com

Library of Congress Cataloging-in-Publication Data
Troupe, Thomas Kingsley.
Quinn and Penny investigate how to research / by Thomas Kingsley Troupe ; illustrated by Sole Otero.
p. cm. – (In the library)
Includes bibliographical references and index.
ISBN 978-1-4048-6290-6 (library binding)
1. Research–Methodology–Juvenile literature. 2. Library research–Juvenile literature. I. Otero, Sole, ill. II. Title.
ZA3080.T76 2011
001.4'2–dc22
2010026894

Printed in the United States of America at Corporate Graphics in North Mankato, Minnesota.
102012 007006R

Meet Quinn and his trusty pen, Penny. Quinn wants to be a detective someday. He knows good detectives ask lots of questions.

Why is the sky blue?
What are fingernails and toenails made of?
How long do crocodiles live?
Does ink wash out of checkered capes?

Step 1—What's the Assignment?

Ms. Readwell gives the class an assignment. "When you research, you look for facts to answer a question. Today I want you to start researching a ***key question.***

KEY QUESTION:
HOW HAS A FAMOUS LEGEND CHANGED OVER TIME?

"Wow!" Quinn says. "You mean a legend like the Loch Ness Monster?"

"Yes," Ms. Readwell says. "You can use information you already know. But you must also come up with new questions to answer."

"What do we do with the information we find?" Quinn asks.

"You'll present it to the class," Ms. Readwell says. "You can make any kind of project."

Our first case!
A good detective asks questions about the assignment. Make sure you know exactly what your task is.

Step 2—Ask Questions and Brainstorm

"Ms. Readwell said we need to make a list of **secondary questions.** A good secondary question helps answer the key question," says Quinn.

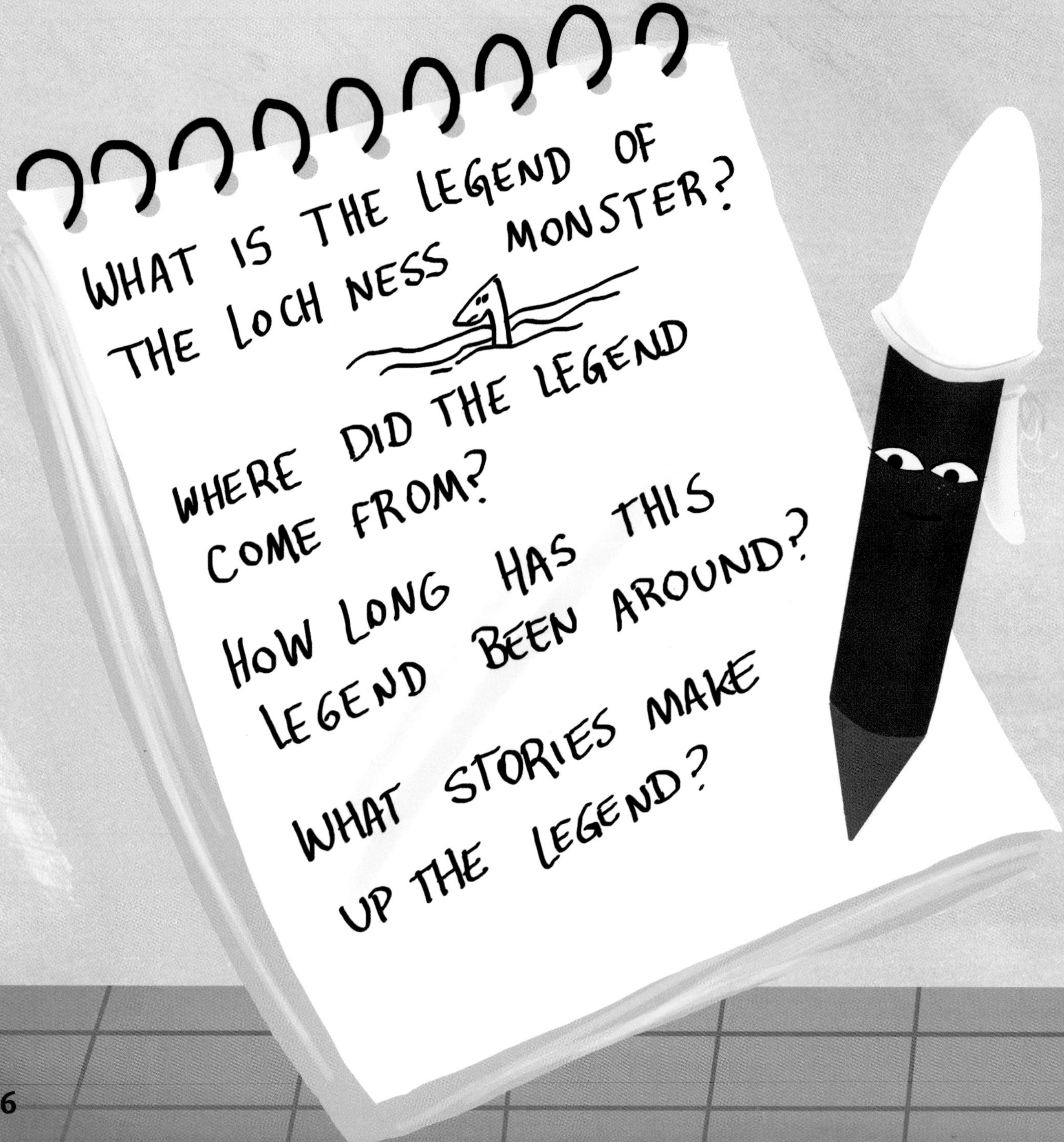

WHAT IS THE LEGEND OF THE LOCH NESS MONSTER?
WHERE DID THE LEGEND COME FROM?
HOW LONG HAS THIS LEGEND BEEN AROUND?
WHAT STORIES MAKE UP THE LEGEND?

Quinn and Penny ***brainstorm*** for their investigation. They think of sources to help them crack the case.

"All this stuff is at the library," Quinn says.

"Good work!" says Penny.

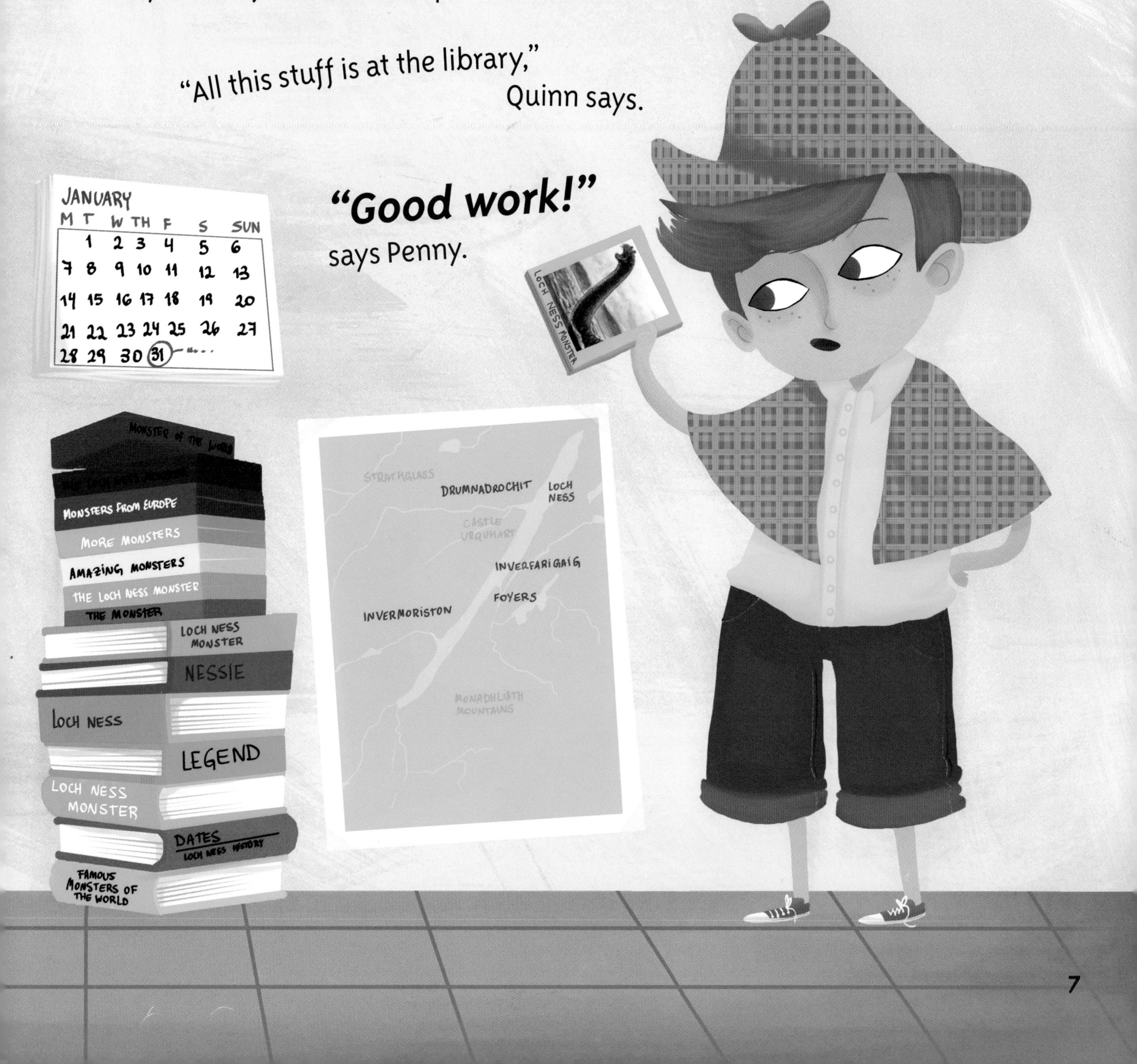

Step 3—Search for Clues

Quinn jots down keywords to help them find **sources** for their case. "Let's do a search for Loch Ness Monster," Quinn says. "Then we'll try the other keywords we have."

Pen-tastic!
There's a book on the Loch Ness Monster.
We're done!

"Not so fast," Quinn says.

"Ms. Readwell said we should check out a bunch of sources.

There are reference books, videos, magazines... all kinds of sources. Let's ask a librarian to help us find some materials."

Penny asks, "How will we ever read all these books, Quinn?"

"The **table of contents** and **index** can help us find facts quickly!" says Quinn.

"We could use the **bibliography** to find other sources too," Penny adds.

Quinn writes down the information he finds. He uses **reference books**, such as encyclopedias, almanacs, and atlases too. These books can't leave the library.

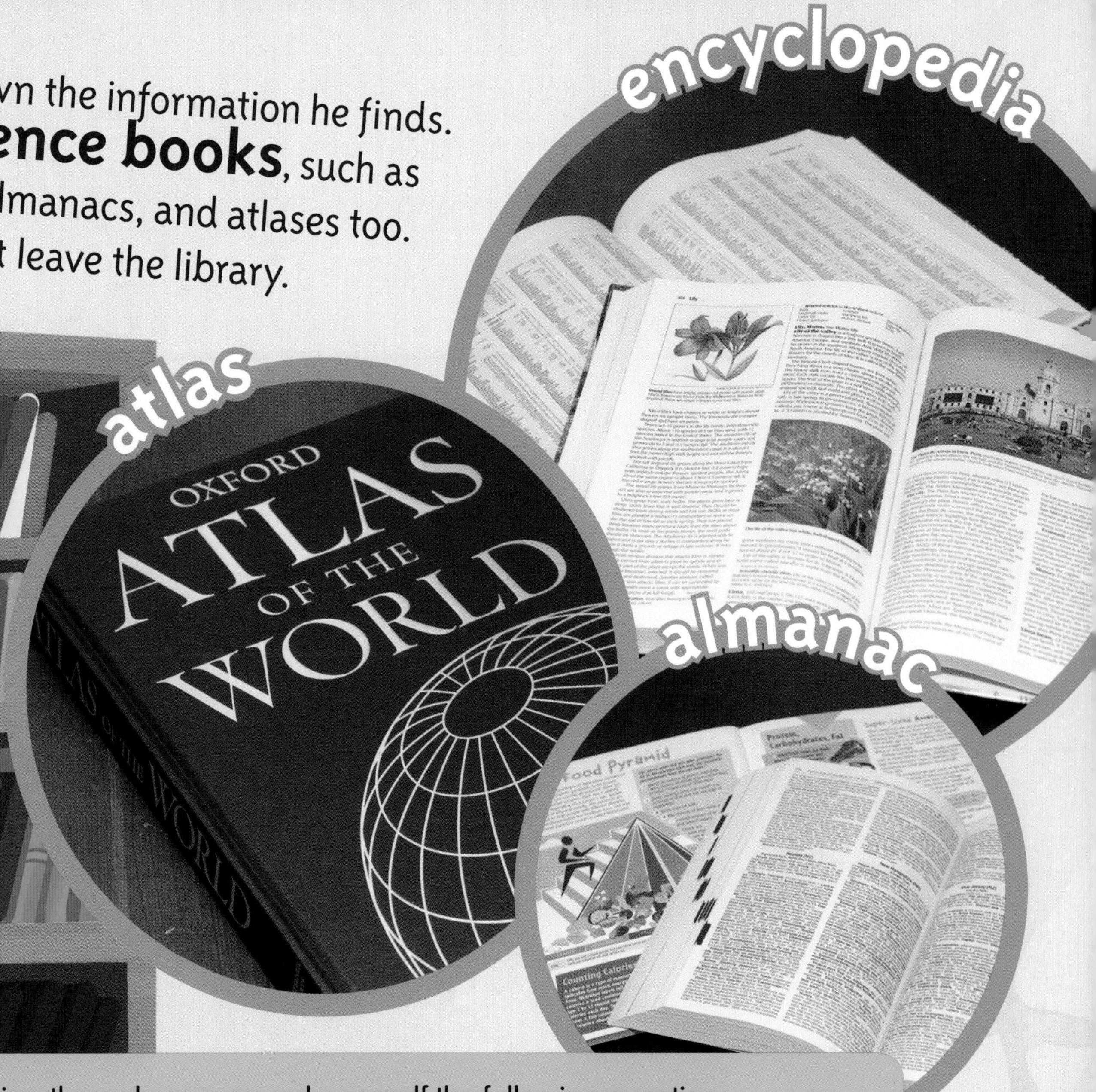

p.36

p.40

p.42

When looking through sources, ask yourself the following questions:

- Is the information in this source answering one of my questions?
- Is the author of the text trustworthy?
- Was this information written to let people know just the facts?
- Was this text written within the last five years?

If you answered yes to all of these questions, your source is likely a good one.

The legend of the Loch Ness Monster leads Quinn and Penny to the computer stations. Quinn uses a popular **search engine** to find Web sites and articles.

"Let's try some other search engines," Quinn says. "We can also use databases. Let's ask the librarian for help too."

This Web site has pictures of Nessie!

Keep track of your sources. It's important to write down the title of the book, Web site, or other source for your report. Ask your teacher what other information you'll need to turn in about your sources.

"Yes, but are they real?" Quinn asks.

"Let's investigate further."

Quinn jots down the Web sites and the useful and trustworthy information. He writes down any other interesting clues he finds.

-The LOCH NESS monster's name is NESSIE
-LOCH NESS is in Scotland
-First account of the Loch Ness Monster was lon
long ago.

Videos

Libraries have more than just books, magazines, and computers. Quinn and Penny find DVDs with **documentaries** about the Loch Ness monster. They bring them to a media station.

"What's a documentary, Quinn?" Penny asks.

"It's a factual movie that shows discoveries other detectives have made," Quinn says.

"Someone else's research?" Penny asks.

"Exactly," Quinn says.

Penny notes the amazing things they see.

"Look at this!" Quinn says.

"Ink-credible! It looks like a dinosaur," Penny says.

Good detectives find information from at least three sources. Try to look at all kinds of sources, such as documentaries, Web sites, newspaper articles, and books. You can also interview people and do surveys for information.

Step 4—Take Notes

Quinn checks out lots of books and DVDs. He knows he and Penny might uncover new clues by reading further.

"I'm tired too," Quinn says.

"We've uncovered a lot of information."

"But did we find enough?" Penny asks. "Let's gather all the facts," Quinn says. Quinn and Penny write everything down.

"Looks like we have plenty of evidence for our case!" Quinn says.

Once the research is done, organize your findings. Writing each piece of information on a note card helps keep things straight. It's important to think about how the information will help answer the key question.

Step 5—Putting It All Together

Quinn and Penny lay out all their note cards on the desk. Then they come up with **answers** to the secondary questions. From those answers, they also **answer the key question.**

How should we show this to the class?

"I know!" Quinn says.

"Let's make a case file, like real detectives!"

Quinn creates an **outline** to use as a guide. Using the outline, Quinn and Penny write a **rough draft** of the case.

Quinn knows he should **never copy** the entire text from a source and turn it in as his own. He rewords their findings and adds new information.

Be creative about how you present your case. Sometimes a report is best. Other times, a video does the trick. Sometimes your teacher will decide the best way to present your facts.

Step 6—Close the Case

Quinn and Penny look at their case file. It's loaded with facts. They add a map of Loch Ness.

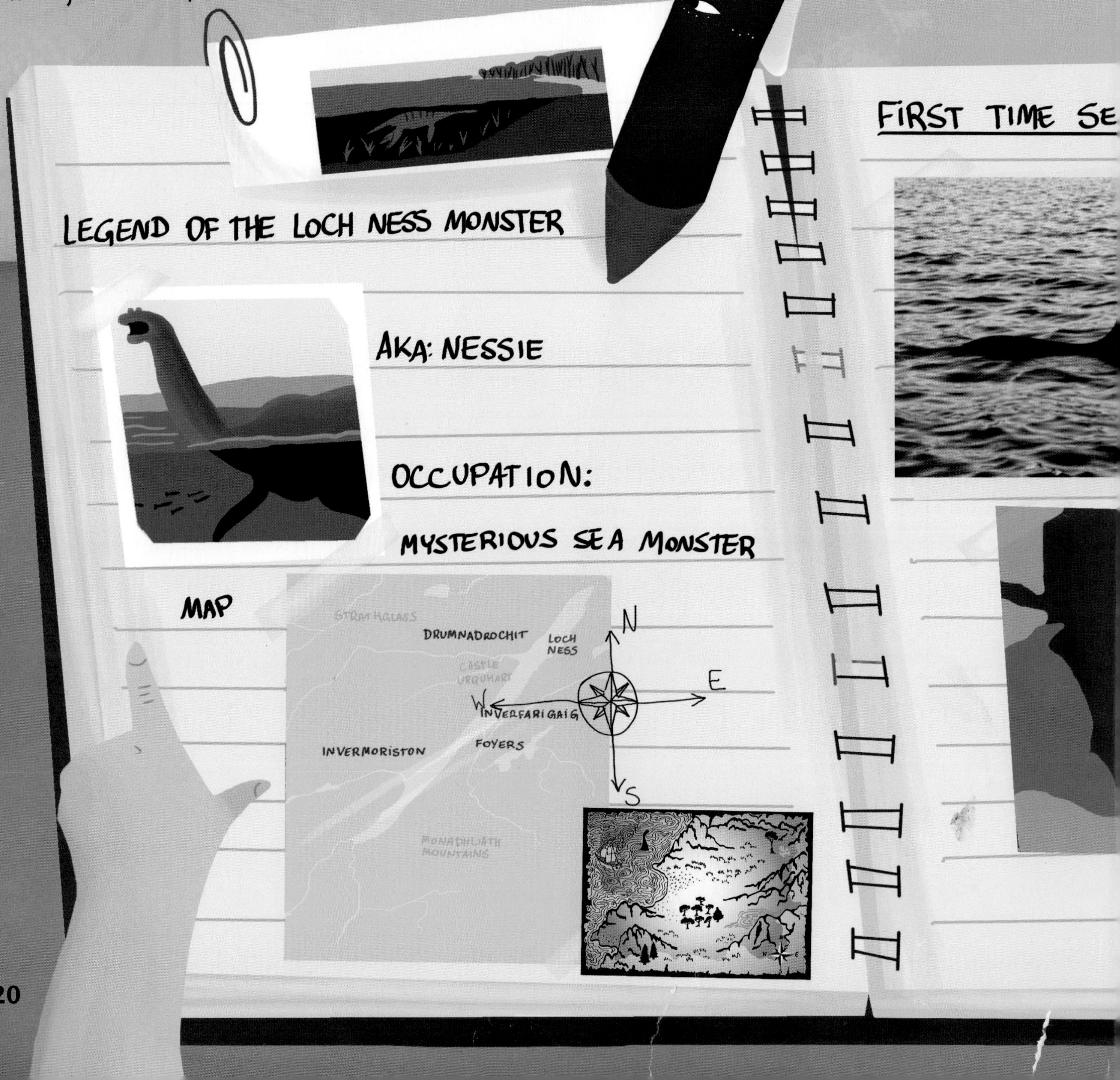

"All the clues were triple checked," Penny says.

"This looks great! We're pretty good detectives," Quinn says.

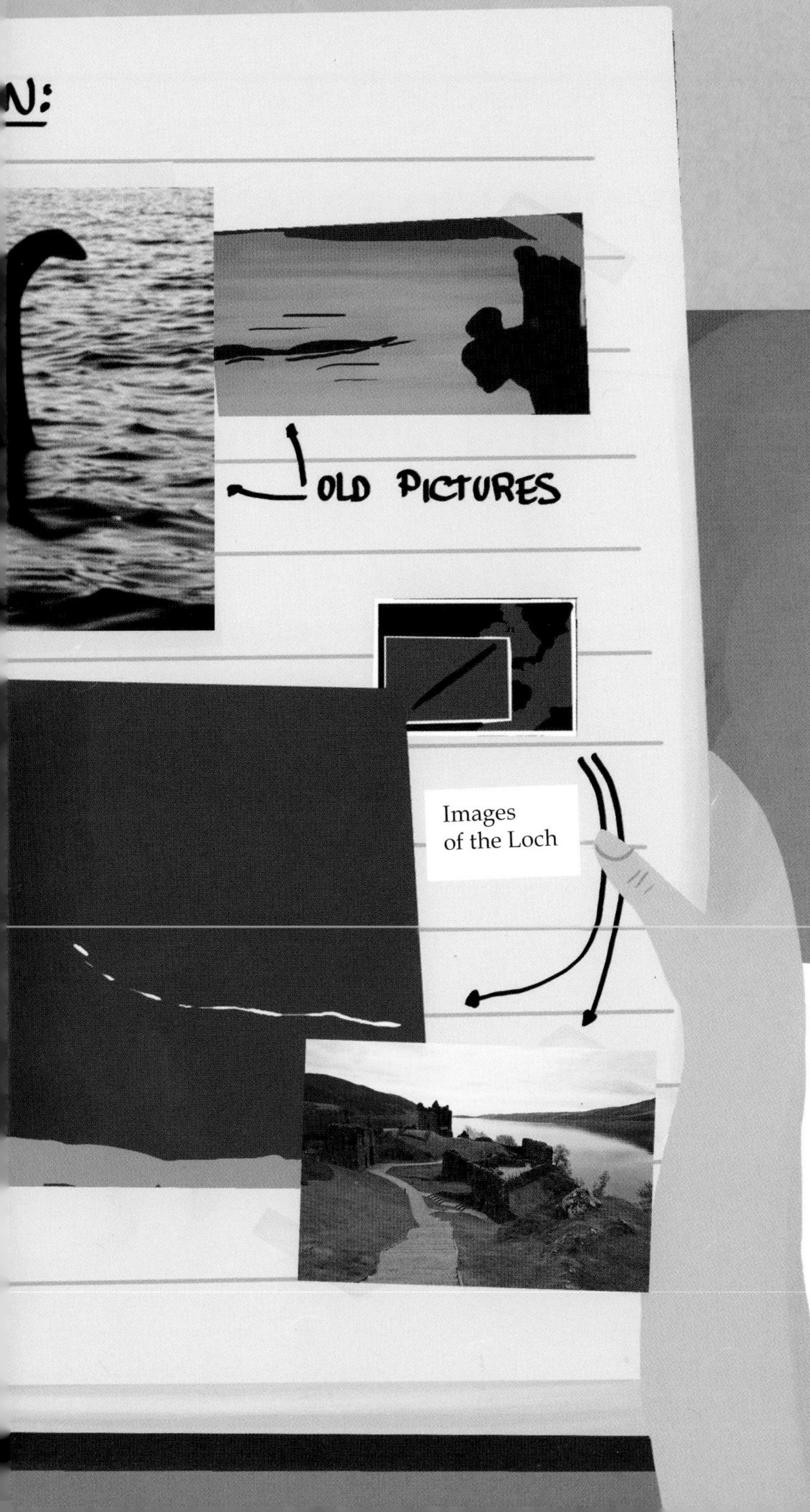

Quinn reads through the case file one last time. Then he and Penny list the sources in a **bibliography.** Next Quinn asks his dad to read the rough draft of the case file. An extra pair of eyes always helps!

It was time to show the case file to the class.

"No one really knows if the Loch Ness Monster is real," Quinn says. "But we sure found a lot of clues. We came up with an answer to the key question too."

"Would you do anything differently for your next case?" Ms. Readwell asks.

"Yes," Quinn says. **"Pick a tougher mystery to solve!"**

Key Question:

How has a famous legend changed over time?

Answer:
The legend of the Loch Ness Monster began more than 1,500 years ago. It started as art and stories. Later it turned into sightings. When people first heard about Nessie, they were scared of her. Now, hundreds of years later, travelers from around the world come to Loch Ness to try and see Nessie for themselves. She has gone from a scary monster to a mysterious creature people love.

Good detectives learn from their past cases. Write in a journal while you are working on your project. Note what would make the next investigation easier. Which sources were most helpful? Did you learn a new way to research? Would you do anything differently?

GLOSSARY

bibliography—a list of sources used to create a book or research paper

brainstorm—to discuss and come up with possible ideas

database—a collection of information on a computer

documentary—a program that shows nonfiction research on a subject

evidence—an item that can prove or disprove something as fact

index—a list of topics covered in a nonfiction book, along with the page numbers on which they are discussed

key question—a question that is essential, or necessary; it is not a yes or no question

legend—a story handed down from earlier times that seems real

outline—a draft that summarizes the main points

reference book—a book that has information arranged in an orderly, convenient way; dictionaries, encyclopedias, atlases, and almanacs are all reference books

research—to study carefully to find and learn facts

rough draft—an early version of a paper; sometimes there are many rough drafts before a final draft is ready

search engine—a program that retrieves information from a database or network

secondary question—a question that helps you answer the key question

source—a book, magazine, article, video, Web site, or person used to provide information in research

table of contents—the page in a book that lists what is found in the main text

MORE BOOKS TO READ

Arnone, Marilyn P. *Mac, Information Detective, in the Curious Kids—Digging for Answers: A Storybook Approach to Introducing Research Skills.* Westport, Conn.: Libraries Unlimited, 2006.

Jakubiak, David J. *A Smart Kid's Guide to Doing Internet Research.* Kids Online. New York: PowerKids Press, 2010.

Miller, Pat. *Research Skills.* Stretchy Library Lessons. Fort Atkinson, Wis.: UpstartBooks, 2003.

INTERNET SITES

FactHound offers a safe, fun way to find Internet sites related to this book. All of the sites on FactHound have been researched by our staff.

Here's all you do:

Visit *www.facthound.com*

Type in this code: 9781404862906

INDEX

LOOK FOR ALL OF THE BOOKS IN THE IN THE LIBRARY SERIES:

* Bob the Alien Discovers the Dewey Decimal System
* Bored Bella Learns About Fiction and Nonfiction
* Karl and Carolina Uncover the Parts of a Book
* Margo and Marky's Adventures in Reading
* Pingpong Perry Experiences How a Book Is Made
* Quinn and Penny Investigate How to Research